MY JOURNEY

MY JOURNEY

THE ME THAT I AM

by
Margaret L. Hyde

Xulon Press

Xulon Press
2301 Lucien Way #415
Maitland, FL 32751
407.339.4217
www.xulonpress.com

© 2020 by MARGARET L. HYDE

All rights reserved solely by the author. The author guarantees all contents are original and do not infringe upon the legal rights of any other person or work. No part of this book may be reproduced in any form without the permission of the author. The views expressed in this book are not necessarily those of the publisher.

Unless otherwise indicated, Scripture quotations taken from the King James Version (KJV) – *public domain*.

Printed in the United States of America.

ISBN-13: 978-1-6628-0319-2

> "THERE BUT FOR THE GRACE OF GOD, GO I"
>
> – JOHN BRADFORD 1553

Contents

HOMES WE LIVED IN   2

SCHOOLS I ATTENDED   6

MY FAMILY   10

MY MOTHER   20

MY JOURNEY   28

THE STRANGER NEXT DOOR   38

THE BATTERED WIFE   42

TRYING TO UNDERSTAND   46

PREMONITION   50

DOMESTIC VIOLENCE   56

I AM WOMAN HEAR ME ROAR   60

FRIENDS AND RELATIONSHIPS   64

AMERICAN ASSOCIATION OF UNIVERSITY WOMEN   70

TRAVEL   74

"THE BOYS" THAT HELPED SAVE A FAMILY   82

PEOPLE WHO INFLUENCED ME   86

HOMES WE LIVED IN

Our first house was a one-room shack in LaFollett, Tennessee just up the mountain from Harriman. If not for the pictures I found in the cedar chest when Mother passed away, I would not have remembered this time of my life at all. In one picture, I can see a water pump so we must have had an out-house in the back. There is nothing but dirt for the yard. We were so far away from anywhere, I have no idea what my father did to support us. I was told that Joe was born at home and weighed around 11 pounds, and there was concern over whether he would live due to breathing problems. I was told that I was born in the hospital, but I have no way of knowing how I got there. I can remember being told I came down the river in a basket which worked pretty well until I got old enough to read the story about Moses. (At times, I think I must have the word STUPID printed on my forehead.)

CHATTANOOGA

Our first "home" in Chattanooga was one room in a large Victorian home on 5th Street above the viaduct. It was the 2nd or 3rd house on the left side of the street. I was 4 years old when we moved into this house. We all slept in the same room. We must have walked down the hall to use the bathroom. I cannot remember, at all, how my Mother prepared our meals or if the lady that owned the house allowed us to eat with her. All I remember is that there were beautiful irises in the yard. (I envy people who have memories back to their births!) I cannot even remember being four years old. I do not know how long we lived in this house.

Our second "home" in Chattanooga was a two-room apartment upstairs at 314 Douglas Street with a screened in porch that we used for a bedroom for Joe and me. It must have had a bathroom, but I cannot remember where it was. The large room included a living area, kitchen, kitchen table with 4 chairs. I do not remember how long we lived in this house either. We must have had some kind of living room furniture and bed. We must have had some kind of stove for heating because I can remember my father falling down the stairs carrying a bucket of hot ashes and burning himself severely. It was one of the few times I saw my father cry. I do not know if he went to the hospital or not. It was at this time I do remember the Salvation Army bringing us baskets at Christmas time, and my father was furious. Apparently, the church had turned in our names. My father would rather we do without food than admit to anyone he could not provide for his family. But no matter how poor we were, my father never went without cigarettes and alcohol.

Our third "home" in Chattanooga was at 501 Baldwin Street. We felt so rich because this house had seven rooms—four downstairs and three upstairs and a bathroom!! We even had an upstairs which meant we were really rich. The rent was about $50 a month for several years, and I can remember when Mother was afraid we would have to move when they raised the rent to $75 a month. We lived on one half of the house and another family lived on the other side. You could see where the connecting doors had been hammered shut. It didn't matter. This was so much bigger than our other home, and it sat right next to the Confederate Cemetery. We lived in this house until my Mother passed away in 1968. I went to Dickinson Junior High from this house. Also, Chattanooga High School. My Aunt Harriet and Uncle A.C. lived with us, off and on, and helped pay the bills.

All three houses are gone now. The last two were taken over by the University of Chattanooga - Tennessee. I would loved to have had the street sign for Baldwin Street, but I never thought of it in time. I have enough memories I guess.

SCHOOLS
I ATTENDED

MISS MCINTYRE'S DAY SCHOOL

When we moved to Chattanooga so that my brother could start school, my Mother went to register Joe into Clara Carpenter Elementary School. When they told my Mother that she would have to pay for all of Joe's books, my Mother found Miss McIntyre's Day School which was only half a block from our house. It is said that God works in mysterious ways, and He sure does. How in the world my Mother got us into the Day School, I will never know. My brother refused to go unless I went with him so I ended up starting school at the age of 4. We could not afford to pay the tuition. I guess, without knowing it, we were provided with tuition free education. I think my Mother promised that my father would do all of the repairs and maintenance at the school to pay for our tuition, but I never saw him at the school the whole time I was there. The grades went from first to twelfth grades, but we went to public junior high in the seventh grade. An exception was made for me, and I went to two years pre-school—long before pre-school was even known. I really should have taken the time to go back and visit the school and thank them for teaching me the love of reading. Miss Matthews was the assistant teacher. Lulu was the black cook. We always went home for lunch since we were so close by. It was a real treat if we got to have lunch at school. Our curriculum was big on language arts, music, art, dancing. I do not remember any math and science, but I'm sure we must have had some.

DICKINSON JUNIOR HIGH

What a shock this was to us! The school was so big compared to our little Day School. And we had so many different classes with so many different teachers. I can remember my math teacher, Miss Coleman, who called my Mother in for a conference because I was getting physically sick every day in her class. To say I hated her class would be an understatement of all times! As far as I was concerned, she could be speaking Greek. I didn't know anything she was talking about. Miss Coleman was tall and extremely thin and wore wire glasses and peered down over them looking at you. I think the 9th grade was my last year for math. I still do not like working with math. Mrs. Ralph was my Science teacher. I didn't know anything she was talking about, but I didn't get sick in her class. She was a rather large woman—rather plump. I managed to survive Science, but it was never my favorite subject. Thank goodness, I had Miss Stegmeyer for physical education because she took me under her wing and introduced me to sports. For that, I will ever be grateful. I finally found something I could do, and she encouraged me to do everything. Even become a class assistant. I had found my forte. Sports got me through junior high and high school. (I wish I had gone back to thank her, too)

CHATTANOOGA HIGH SCHOOL OR CITY HIGH

I continued participating in sports. Although I stayed to myself pretty much in high school, I did work my way up in the Drill Squad until I was second in command. I lettered in volleyball, softball, and tennis. I was a sponsor for the R.O.T.C. and was elected to the May Day court. The best thing though was when I was elected to represent my homeroom on the Student Council.

SCHOOLS I ATTENDED

I couldn't believe it because we had the cutest girl, Barbara Watts, in my class, and I knew she would win it for sure. I was so happy. However, I still ran to the closest door at the west entrance of the school so that I could be the first one out the door and managed to run through the cemetery and hide in my house before the other kids walked by and saw where I lived. I was so ashamed of where I lived, and I really believed that I could hide so that the other kids didn't know where I lived! Talk about being naïve and stupid!

When I graduated from City High School, I was offered a tennis scholarship to Bernau College in Georgia. Even with the scholarship, it was too expensive. Besides, my Mother figured that I was getting too serious with Bob Sharpe who was going to Georgia Tech so I was sent in the opposite direction to U.T. Bob was a Christian Scientist and Mother didn't approve of that. Funny, I wonder how many times she regretted that decision. Bob went on to become a very successful engineer and lives in Atlanta. (p.s.) When I was in junior high, I had a real big crush on Joe Spector who lived in the house on the other side of our duplex. It was nothing serious. Just a teen-age crush because he went away to Georgia Tech while I was in junior high. The family was Orthodox Jewish so Joe honored the traditions. He could not eat anything that wasn't "kosher" like the cookies I would make for him. He was so tall and good-looking. I learned later that he died in his 30's from a heart attack.

So, I have often wondered how different my life would have been if I had gone to Bernau College, but I will never know. Hindsight is so much better and more effective than foresight!

MY FAMILY

My family was made up of a father, mother, brother and me. At that time, it was considered a "typical family". Our family was not "typical" at all. My mother was intelligent and, for the period, well-educated. At a time when young people dropped out of school in the 8th grade so that they could go to work and help support the family, all of the children in my mother's family graduated from high school and, for some reason, most of them were ambitious. They lived on a piece of land that had been handed down as a land grant from the Revolutionary War. Since the government could not pay the soldiers for their services, they rewarded them with land grants. My Grandfather Holloway was a butcher in the only grocery store in the small town of Spring City, Tennessee with a population of less than 2,000. The family did not have much money, but they always had food from the grocery store and from Grandmother's garden.

Over the years, the family had to sell off some of the land to pay taxes. The town bought enough land to build the high school's football field and the city park. In the 1990's, the state decided to widen Highway U.S. 27which meant the state would take over Grandmother Holloway's house which was over 120 years old and the surrounding property near the road. After that, the family only had eight acres left so they decided to donate the land to the town of Spring City to use as a soccer field.

My father's family was different. He, too, came from a family of eight children. I do not know how many graduated from high school. We did not visit their family very often. At the time, I thought it was because it was so hard to get to their home since it was located on the side of the mountain outside of Harriman, Tennessee. However, as I reflect back on the time, I think it may have been because all of the boys in the family were alcoholic and my mother wanted to avoid the situation. Grandmother Whalen was a very thin, stern person who belonged to the WCTU (Women's Christian Temperance Union or something like that). She was very much opposed to drinking. I do not think any of the girls drank at all, but all four boys were alcoholics. One of the "boys" was shot in a near-by bar and paralyzed, from the waist down, for the rest of his life. Another one of the "boys" ran moonshine. It was always rumored that his house sat on the county line so that whenever the sheriff from one county would come to arrest him, he would put the moonshine on the other side of the house! I do not remember Grandfather Whalen at all.

My mother really deserved someone better, but my father was the only man she ever "knew", and they had a shotgun wedding. Many times she wished she was not married, but divorce was out of the question. In fact, many years later, when my first cousin got the first divorce in the family, no one in the family spoke to her for years. She helped pave the way for me several years later. As I look back on it now, I wonder if part of the reasons not to get a divorce was so that you didn't have to admit you were wrong. Certainly, if my mother had been alive, I would not have gotten a divorce. During my mother's lifetime, it could have also been because of economics. My mother could never have moved back home with two children. (I have often wondered what our lives would have been like if we had grown up surrounded and supported by our family.)

My brother, Joe, was two years older than me and, in our family, the boys were always the "chosen" ones. I think this reflects back on the time when, in the south, a family could own more property if they had the boys to farm it. Even though our society is getting better at it, my Grandmother Holloway made a special trip to visit us in Knoxville when our son was born. (It may also have been because the trip was more feasible than Texas.) I still cannot remember how she got there because my family still did not have a car. I am amazed at how much travel we did by bus. We were lucky because the bus stopped right next to the dorms at U.T. My parents had to borrow a car to pick me up after my graduation. (We did not have a car until 1961 when my parents bought a used 1958 Ford).

My brother, Joe, the "first born" could do no wrong growing up, and I could do nothing right. (I'm sure he would disagree with me.) After he passed away, I wished that we had talked more because Joe remembered so much about our growing up and where everyone lived, etc. I had spent my lifetime trying to forget. Joe was always outgoing and friendly. The real "class clown". He was also really talented in singing. He always sang in the chorus in high school and college. He played football, baseball and tennis in high school. Somehow, my mother was able to get him a scholarship to Tennessee Wesleyn College a Methodist college in Cleveland, Tennessee where he continued to play tennis and had the lead in several of the musicals.

After junior college, Joe decided to go into the Air Force. I do not know why. I guess he wanted to get out on his own. I can still see him walking off to the recruitment center in downtown Chattanooga. Neither one of our parents went with him. He was never the same Joe ever again. I do not know what he saw or what he did in the Air Force, but he came home quiet, reclusive, "dark" and an alcoholic. He started running around with the wrong crowd and started to gamble in "joints". There were bars with illegal gambling along the Tennessee River, and he worked as a bartender in one of them. Apparently, somewhere he crossed up with some pretty bad people because someone blew up his truck while it was parked outside my mother's house. He lived pretty much in fear after that. (When eating out in public, neither my father or Joe would never sit with their backs to the front door.) It was neurotic behavior probably a result of their alcoholism or all of their gambling. They must have been afraid of being caught by someone or something.

After serving in the Air Force, Joe would work enough and save money so that he could move out of mother's house. Then, when he ran out of money, he would move back into mother's house and start all over again. One time, he was the number #1 used car salesman in Hamilton County. Not just in Chattanooga, but the whole county. But, alcohol always came back to haunt him.

Joe was married for a while and had a baby girl, Stephanie. Joe told me later on that he would never have named her that if he thought Stacy's name was Stephanie. I never figured out if this was a compliment or not. When our mother died, he bought a little house on an acre of land in Ringgold, Georgia. There he lived with 6-8 dogs and cats. At one time, he even had a skunk! It must have terrified him to know that he no longer had anyone to fall back on. He managed for several years, but then he decided to walk out losing the house and his car when he only owed about $5,000 to pay off the house. I would have gladly paid off the house so that he could have a place to live, but he walked out leaving all of our childhood pictures, memories, furniture, clothing and things that meant so much to the family. He even left all of the trophies and medals we had won. They meant nothing to him, and I doubt if he ever looked back.

After losing his house and car, he moved in with his ex-wife and her new husband while they had moved back home to live with her mother. Hard to believe, when you think about it, but I guess he didn't think he had any other place to go. And they let him move in! The house was a big, old ranch style home and Joe lived on one side, and everyone else lived on the other side. To justify living there, Joe agreed to cut the grass and clean up the outside. This was to pay for his room and board. He would not come out of his room to eat, so his ex-mother-in-law brought his meals to his room. Talk about "enabling"! It finally got so bad that his ex-mother-in-law threatened to have the sheriff come and remove him. I am amazed that Barbara, his ex-wife, allowed him to move in.

When he finally moved out from his ex-wife's house, he moved into his daughter Stephanie's car. Yes, he slept in the car at night and then he would drive Stephanie to work so that he could use her car to drive to the Elk's Club to shave and clean up. I have no idea what he did all day long, but he would pick up Stephanie at the end of her work day, drive her home, and go back to sleep in her car. The apartment manager finally told Stephanie that she could not allow her father to sleep in her car, and if he continued she would have to move out.

At this point, Stephanie put Joe on a bus and shipped him to live with me in Florida! When Joe arrived, everything he owned was in his old duffel bag. I was working full time and had a lot on my plate. Apparently, Joe had made the decision 10-11 years before that he didn't want to work anymore. I didn't know you had a choice. I told him that as long as he lived with me, he would have to do some kind of work. I didn't care what he did. If he would work 3-4 days a week, I would match what he made and he could live anywhere he wanted to live. (I even drove Joe by several apartments where he could live.) Joe arrived on Sunday and on Thursday he had a job as a bagger at a near-by grocery store so he could walk. We had to go to the clothing store to get him pants, shirt and shoes to wear to work.

We had problems from the beginning. Apparently, everywhere he lived he could smoke as much as he wanted... in the house! I have never figured out how people who have no money at all always have money for cigarettes. Joe smoked 2-3 packs of cigarettes every day, and I am allergic to smoke. Joe would smoke on the front porch. He did not realize that the smoke blew into the house and his clothes reeked of smoke. One early morning, while he was smoking on the front porch in the dark, he yelled at one of the neighbors and scared him. The neighbor was running and had decided to turn around in the driveway. Joe was distrustful of everyone.

After about 4-5 months, we were able to move Joe into subsidized housing. Here, again, I reminded him that if he would work for 3-4 days, I would match it, and he told me he never wanted to work again. When he moved out of my house, he never worked again. He did have some pride, though, he refused to accept the food stamps he qualified for. He was living on his Social Security check. I told him that he would qualify for SSI, if he would check "mentally ill" on the form! That got his attention! He said there was no way he was "mentally ill", and I told him that there was no way someone could just quit work and expect someone else to take care of him. It was a attitude I couldn't afford.

I went around to all of our friends and relatives and got enough furniture to furnish his small apartment size unit in Dunedin. One friend even donated a bicycle. For a while, he enjoyed riding his bicycle on the Pinellas Trail. He lived in Dunedin for 10 years. He enjoyed a few good years. Towards the end, I doubt if he could have worked, but he could have worked a few years. He was always fearful that someone from his past would find him so his telephone was unlisted. In order to speak to him over the phone, you had to call, let the phone ring two times, hang up, then dial again. This took a long time –especially when I was in Colorado and calling with a calling card. If I didn't time it just right, he wouldn't pick up. The timing had to be just right so that Joe knew it was the same person calling. Joe often referred to his housing as "the compound". I reminded him that the other people living there were there because they had to. He was living there because he chose to. He chose to stay by himself. Even a man living behind him, named Bob, tried to be a friend, but I guess he tried to get too close. I had hoped the Joe would marry the lady across the street who showed some interest, but he never gave it a thought. Probably thought she was interested in his money!

Joe was able to live on his Social Security and some money from a settlement from an asbestos company that his neighbors help him fill out the form in order to collect. With this money, he was able to buy a truck which he enjoyed. After he purchased the truck, he never rode his bicycle again. He told me that he had saved about $2,000 which was hidden in his apartment. He would not tell me where—guess he was afraid I would steal it. He also told me he had a safety deposit box where he kept our father's ring. When he died, Stephanie searched the whole place and couldn't find any money, and I wrote the State Department, and they couldn't find any record of a safe deposit box in his name. Hiding money in your house was quite a common thing for people growing up in the depression. Maybe we should name the pattern the "depression syndrome". It was a result of the fear of not having any money. When my mother passed away, we found bills hidden inside the encyclopedias. It is something you never overcome. To this day, I always keep spare money in the house. If Joe did hide any money, it was gone by the time Stephanie got there. Joe was alone when he died. The baseball bat he kept by the front door, as a safety measure in case someone broke in, was still there.

Joe's next door neighbor did not see him for several days so she called the Sheriff's Department. They did not perform an autopsy. Apparently, there are so many seniors in Pinellas County who die alone it would be impossible to perform an autopsy on all of them unless there is a sign of a homicide or something illegal. (I was working in Colorado and waiting for my car to be picked up because it was giving me a lot of problems, and I did not feel safe to drive it home. Joe Daughtery, at Dimmitt Cadillac, had the car picked up and flew me home.) While in Colorado, I called and spoke to the Sheriff who was at Joe's apartment, and he told me that Joe had internal bleeding and cirrhosis of the liver even though he did not drink much towards the end. Apparently, Joe had gone to the emergency room on July 31st. He must have been in pain, or afraid, because he would never go to the hospital otherwise. When the people at the hospital told Joe that they wanted to run tests, Joe got up and left. He died less than a month later. I called him a day or two before he died, and he was very upset because I had promised I wouldn't call until I got home. For some reason, I felt that I needed to call Joe that day. I am glad we got to talk.

As it turned out, Joe was given a military funeral, taps, flag and everything. He was buried in the National Cemetery in Chattanooga with the government paying most of the bills. Thank goodness, Stephanie was able to do this. She had forgotten that Joe had been in the service. When I called her to help with the obituary article for the paper, I reminded her that Joe had been in the service. Joe had always wanted to be buried next to our family in Spring City, but there was no way Stephanie could afford it. I'm just glad that Stephanie could do it this way. Besides Stephanie, Gigi and Finley, there was only one car salesman there for the funeral.

MY FAMILY

My Mother died of breast cancer complications at 59. My Father died as a result of a fall of four stories on a construction job at the age of 59. His supervisor told us he was working in an area where he was not supposed to be and that he had been drinking. We never thought to question his supervisor about the accident, but we never doubted that he would be drinking.

So you can see, we were not a typical family. No family with an alcoholic can ever be normal, typical family

MY MOTHER

This chapter has been more difficult to write and very emotional. I feel that both my brother and me were big disappointments to our Mother. I know I failed God, but it hurt more that I failed Mother.

Looking back in life with a better perspective, I realize that my Mother deserved a better life. I do not know how she managed to do as well as she did. And she tried. She really tried. She reminded us, always, that even though we were poor we could be clean.

We moved down off the mountain when I was four years old and my brother was six. Everything we owned was in one old suitcase wrapped with rope and a cardboard box wrapped in strings. Our first "home" was a rented room in a big, old Victorian home on 5th Street above the viaduct. We must have walked down the hall to go to the bathroom, but I cannot remember how we prepared any meals. I have not idea how my Mother found this place, but it was within walking distance to the grocery store and a pharmacy. We could also walk to town which was a good thing since we had to walk anywhere we wanted to go. The house is gone now and has been gone for a long time. (I have no memories of this time in my life. If there were any pictures, they were lost when my brother left his house with everything in it.)

When we moved to Chattanooga, my Mother went to register my brother into Clara Carpenter Elementary School. (This may be why we moved off the mountain when we did.) My Mother did not realize it at the time, but the students had to buy all of their schoolbooks. We could not afford it. One half block from our rented room sat a day school called Miss McIntyre's Day School. Somehow, my Mother was able to have us admitted as scholarship students by promising that my Father would do all the maintenance and repair work for the school. Yes, God does work in mysterious ways. The day school was in her home, and she had one assistant Miss Matthews. She also had a black cook, Lulu, who prepared lunch for the students. We attended school at Miss McIntyre's until we graduated into the 7th grade. The only memories I have of the school is the beautiful sunroom on the south side of the first floor where we performed our dances, plays, etc. We were allowed to eat at the school only on special occasions because we could walk home for lunch. (And we couldn't afford it.) Because we had lead such a sheltered life and were never allowed to meet other people, my brother refused to go to school unless I went along, So Miss McIntyre allowed me to attend, probably the only time ever, pre-school at the age of 4. (This behavior pattern of isolation still holds true back in the mountains.)

I can remember a very small enrollment at McIntyre's Day School. However, in a picture taken at a later date, I notice there are 21 students enrolled from First Grade through Eighth Grade. I recognize only one other student in the middle of the second row: Georgene Lawson. I called Gigi, who thank goodness, knew who Georgene was married to. She was really surprised when I called her. I made a copy of the picture and sent it to her to see if she recognized anyone else. She had stayed at McIntyre's through the ninth grade. I do not know why Joe is not in the picture because he was a year behind Georgene.

Somehow, my Mother always managed. When we moved to 314 Douglas Street, we had two rooms in an up-stairs arrangement in a house. My Mother, being the eldest of eight children was a wonderful cook, and she could cook a wonderful meal with almost nothing to prepare with. I do not remember how long we lived in this apartment. We must have had a cooking stove or a fireplace because I can remember my father falling down the stairs and burning himself badly with the ashes. It was one of the two times I can remember my father crying. It must have been a cook stove. Surely, I would remember a fireplace, and I cannot remember one in this apartment. (This house is gone, too. The University of Chattanooga bought up all this property for their campus.)

Next, we moved to 501 Baldwin Street where we lived until my Mother passed away. This was big. We were rich. Our new "house" had two floors! Apparently, the house was divided into two sections so that the owner could rent out to two families. That was all right with us. We had seven rooms with four on the first floor and three on the second floor. And our very own bathroom.

I cannot remember how old we were when we moved into this house. I have fond memories of our Mother taking us to the City Library every Saturday for Story House. I am sure this is one of the reasons I love to read so much. And we could get out of doing chores if we were reading a book! I became an avid reader!

After we moved to 501 Baldwin Street, my Mother took a job as a playground director at a near-by city park—Citizen's Park which would become our home until I graduated from high school. She was perfect for the job, and the job was perfect for her. It was opened only in the summertime, and she could keep an eye on us. As the playground director, she was responsible for organizing all of the activities. She had us doing everything. After a while, though, my brother and I focused on tennis.

Somehow, we were in the right place at the right time because a lot of the city tennis championships always came from Citizens. We played tennis four to five hours a day. There were only two clay courts so we had to play "winners only" could stay on the courts. That made it even more competitive.

Our neighborhood was rough and several of our friends ended up being killed. I forget how old I had to be before I could go to the grocery store by myself. I wonder, sometimes, where we would have ended up if not for sports. In high school Joe played football, baseball and tennis. I played volleyball, basketball, volleyball and tennis. Throughout it all, there was our Mother watching over us. My Mother was always active in PTA so she knew what was going on in school, and she was very active in Church so our lives were filled with school and Church activities. One of my saddest memories is when I lost my first tennis match when I was a senior in high school, and my father didn't want to be the one to tell my Mother. It broke her heart. I didn't lose a match in college.

When our rent at 501 Baldwin Street was raised to $75 a month, my Mother was afraid we would have to move. We had never paid more than $50 a month. Somehow, she managed to pull us through so that we were able to stay. It was always my Mother who had to assume responsibility for everything. My father was an alcoholic, and the only thing he worried about was getting drunk every week-end. He never worried about paying bills or having food on the table.

My Mother did not work outside of the home until my brother went off to college. Somehow, probably through our church, my Mother was able to get my brother into Tennessee Wesleyn in Cleveland which was a Methodist junior college. When Joe went away from home, Mother must have suffered something that is known today as "empty nest syndrome" because the doctor recommended that she go to work. She had devoted her entire life to her children.

MY MOTHER

Without any previous experience, she started working at Miller Bros. (like Maas Bros.). She always worked in the office, and she was very good with figures. She had to walk both ways into town, and she always wore heels. Every afternoon, after work, she had to stop at the Red Food Store and pick up food for supper. The store was downtown, and she would have to carry the groceries all the way home. I would say it was at least two and a half to three miles each way. She always came in the door with a bag of groceries. Then she had to prepare supper for the family. The year she died, after working in the store for over 20 years, her income was less than $4,000 a year. I don't know how she managed.

My Mother was very active in church and made sure we were there every Sunday morning for Sunday School and Church and again on Sunday night for youth group. We went to Trinity Methodist Church for as long as I can remember. Church played a very important part in our lives, and I am happy that Mother had the friends that she had at church and at work.

I still do not know how Mother made it possible for me to go to the University of Tennessee. We did not own a house or a car to use as collateral for a loan. There was no money for us to go to college. She always wanted a better life for Joe and me, and she felt the only way out of the gutter was with a good education. After she died, I found the papers where some bank had loaned her money on "the furniture in our house." My Mother valued education very much, and she made many sacrifices for us.

My Aunt Harriet and Uncle A.C. lived with us on Baldwin Street at different times and helped pay the bills. Mother found a neighbor, Mrs. Lawson, who sewed all of my clothes since we could not afford to buy them. It wasn't until my brother and I were both out of school that my Mother was finally able to buy some nice things for herself. I am glad that she had a few years to get some nice things. She always had to put it on lay-away and pay for it over a period of time. My Mother loved to dress up and look nice. She would dress up for church and wear heels even though it was further to walk to Church than it was to walk to town.

I do not know how my Mother was able to find someone to sponsor us for the Chattanooga Tennis Club which was very fancy. After we graduated from Citizens Park, we had a benefactor who paid our memberships in the tennis club until we were out of school. We never knew who it was. Alex Gerry was the President of the Tennis Club and on the Board of the Southern Lawn Tennis Association, and he got me place on the squad from the south ranking #4. It was political even back then, but I didn't realize it.

When I went to Philadelphia to play on the nationals, I do not remember how I got there or playing tennis. The only thing I remember is that the house where I stayed had two different kinds of cereal! I had never seen that before!

Everyone said I was so naïve growing up. Actually, I was painfully shy. My Mother was always there pushing Joe and me. Over Labor Day week-end in 2006, Stephanie showed me pictures of Joe when he went into the Air Force. I had forgotten how good-looking Joe was. They say boys go into the military and come out men. I know of two that went into the military and came out broken. Joe came out an alcoholic and a gambler. The other one who came out broken was my Uncle Woody. He, too, went into the military a happy, easy-going person, but he spent too many years working in the psychiatric ward with patients who came back from World War II. Woody was never the same.

In later years, when my Mother finally saved enough money to buy a used car, I think she was afraid to buy it because she thought that my father would drive while he was drunk and hurt someone. She finally broke down and bought one in 1961. It was a used one. A 1958 Ford. You would have sworn it was a Cadillac. It made Mother so happy. She no longer had to walk to work. My father died in a fall later that year. I hope that Mother got to enjoy the car the few years that she had it. She was diagnosed with breast cancer in 1963 and died in 1968. She worked until May 1968 and died in September. She had a few years to enjoy the car, but she was never able to fulfill her dream of owning a house.

MY JOURNEY

Domestic Violence is still here!

According to the news, domestic violence has gone up during this virus event. It also goes up during the Super Bowl.

What can we, as a society, do to help these young girls realize that they don't have to put up with it. They have choices. They have support groups. They have families.

My generation was different. We had no choice. To admit to my family that I was pregnant and not married would bring shame on the family. And I could never admit to my Mother that I was pregnant. Not after all of the sacrifices my Mother made so that I could have a better life! She would make today's "helicopter" mother look lazy.

My Mother gave new meaning to "make do". We moved off of the mountain when my older brother, Joe, turned six and needed to start school. We had lived in a one room house, set up on concrete blocks, with a water pump in the front and an outhouse in the back. Our yard was dirt. We carried everything we owned in an old beat up suitcase held together with a rope. I do not remember how we got off the mountain. A friend must have driven us.

When my Mother went to register Joe at Clara Carpenter Elementary. she was told that she would have to buy all of Joe's books. My Mother got up and walked out. She knew she could not buy books. There was a private day school in a house down the street, and she walked down and promised the headmaster that, if she would let Joe attend school there, my father would do all of the repairs for the house. And she agreed. On the day Joe was to start school, he refused to go unless I went. (We were the only people we knew). So Miss McIntyre allowed me to go as a four year old. We attended the school until we were in the seventh grade. We went from a small school of 14-15 students to junior high where we had 28 kids in one room.

This was quite a shock. I met 2 girls the entire year. One was named Bonnie and the other was Faye. Needless to say, our social skills were very limited. I became a "nerd: before it was a word. My brother was out going and the class clown. The teacher would cringe when I told her my name. She thought I would be like Joe. My brother attended the school for six years, and I attended for eight. It was several years later that I realized it was a liberal arts school. We read a lot, spelled a lot, gave plays and danced a lot. We had a beautiful sunroom for our activities. I have to admit I do not remember any math or science. But we loved school!

Junior high was not a pleasant part of my life. I had three teachers I remember: Miss Coleman, math; Miss Ralph, science and Miss. Stagmeyer, P.E. teacher and a god-send. She took me under wings and got me involved in sports: tennis, volley ball, soft ball and basketball I am thankful everyday for her influence. We had always gone home for lunch. I know they didn't have free lunches so our Mother must have packed our lunch. The most I can say about junior high is that I survived it!

Up until this time, we always had one room only for all four of us. The fourth house had a kitchen! Mother thought we were rich because we had a kitchen. I cannot remember how she fixed our food because I can't remember eating. This house was like half a house. Someone locked the connecting doors so we had half with a living room, dining room, kitchen and three rooms upstairs and one bathroom. My parents lived the rest of their lives there at 501

Baldwin St. Right next to the Confederate Cemetery. The only bad thing was that all of the high school students walked by our house. So I planted myself near the exit so that when the bell rang, I was home and hid out before the rest of the school got there.

I guess you could say I "bloomed" in high school. I was on the drill team and worked my way up to Major, second in command. Someone in R.O.T.C. chose me to be his sponsor. I continued to be active in sports where I focused on tennis. There was a city playground neat the house, and when we go got old enough to go there our Mother worked as a director, and I don't know if she got paid, but she was there everyday. This playground produced several city champions and several of us were invited to play at the tennis club. I do not know who paid our memberships, but we were lucky. My brother and I were City Champions several years. The competition was so great that you could only stay on the court if you won. If you lost, you had to go sit down. One of the members went on to coach tennis at the University of Tennessee, and another one became a pro at the club on the mountain. I credit sports for keeping us out of trouble.

The President of the Tennis Club was also President of the Southern Junior Tennis League so I got to play there. (When I lost my first match, as a senior in high school, my father could not tell my Mother so I had to.) Tennis was for winning. I played tennis in college for my sorority and won points for them. I think that is why they wanted me. When I left college, I did not pick up a racquet until my children were in middle school. Then I played on different teams at the club. I would like to say I played for fun, but it was always competition for me.

When I went away to college, I had to be the most stupid, naive, freshman ever to go. My first year I stayed in the freshman dorm.

Which was good. We had a 9:15 curfew. After that, I lived in a smaller, less expensive dorm. I worked in the Dean of Women's Office for spending money. And, also, at a dress shop where I got a discount and got to model. My Mother always taught me that, if you look deep enough, you can always find the good in everybody. I am glad she did not live long enough to see how I ended up in college.

Reading. I became an avid reader when I realized that if I was reading, my Mother would not ask me to do chores! To this day, I never go anywhere without a book!

The first person I met, on campus, was pure evil. My Mother did not teach me about evil. She always taught me "if you look deep enough, you can find the good in everybody", I am glad she did not live long enough to find out it's not true. I did not date until I was a senior in high school, and the only boys I dated were from church or school. Of course, the first thing the evil one introduced me to—was alcohol. From there, it was downhill the whole way. He told me that he loved me. That was him first lie. Then he convinced me that no one else would have me. For someone with poor self-esteem. he had me convinced. If I had not been so stupid and naive, I would not have believed him.

I didn't pledge a sorority until my third year when I, finally, made it in to the one I wanted. I was not a legacy, and I had no one at home to recommend me. I think I, finally, got in because of my abilities in sports. and I could win points that way. Some goal I never understood, but I know we came in twice, two different times, so it was good. We did not have sorority houses so I continued to live in the small building across the street from the campus.

I had several honors in college, but they are meaningless now. After going with the same person for four years, I was still ignorant of life. I do not know why anyone did not tell me. To this day, I do not have anyone close to talk to. That is the first thing you learn about domestic violence. You are not allowed anyone to support you. In fact, the key word is "control". When I got pregnant, I had no choice like the girls do now. I had to get married or bring shame on my family. I cannot tell you how many times I wish I had taken the shame, but I could never admit, to my Mother, that I was pregnant and not married. So we got married.

I cannot say it was a "blessed" marriage, but we had a family, and I was brought up to believe that the family comes first. A family is a lot like a baseball team. In order to function, everyone on the team has to participate. I will not say that my "then" husband was perfect, but after he began the affair with one of his high school students, he turned his back on us forever. This would have been a perfect time to give me and the kids a divorce and freedom from his abuse, but only an honorable man would do such a thing, and no one ever accused him of being "honorable".

Adultery must be exciting, thrilling. Otherwise, why would anyone choose to hide, sneak around, lie, and give up his family? And never look back? He tossed us out like you throw out the garbage. He forced us to carry on, like before, because there was no way he was going to give up my income and his four slaves (children). the only time he wanted them was when there was work to do. He was never a father to them or a supportive spouse to me. The abuse, alone, was enough, but to find out he had a (girlfriend, whore, mistress) whatever they call them now was too much to bear. She knew all along that he was married. So did he!

MY JOURNEY

They started the affair around 1965. By the time he got a divorce, which took seven years. He made sure all of our investments were gone. The divorce became final in 2002. For some reason, our papers were sealed. So they kept all of my salary for 25 years that he took to invest in "our" future. He forgot to tell me I would not be there. They took all of the money our children had worked for and done without for. The crowning blow came when he had always promised to build the house of my dreams, he told me that if I would buy all of the materials, he would build it for me. However, when it came time for me to get the house, I would have to come up with $40,000. He knew I could not do that so he said he would give me the money and buy the house. Think about it, a two story house, completely furnished and landscaped for $40,000.00, Unheard of. To make matters worse, it took him four years to do it. He did not give me four years to do it. Please do not ask me why I believed him when he had lied to me and the kids all of our lives.

We were professional people. That is not how a professional person acts. My then-husband was a "con," and he taught his girlfriend that it was easier to take then it was to earn. She had no problems taking our life savings and money that the kids had been promised, I didn't think it was possible, but my then-husband found someone just like him!

I realize that people say "life is not fair", but surely common decency is fair. They lied, cheated, stole, and hid everything. I doubt if anyone could find it. So much for common decency.

I would like to think I can teach other young girls to know better. Today, they have a choice, and yet I still hear about domestic violence. They have support groups, church support, professions support and they now have shelters. Of course, the first thing you have in domestic violence is complete control by the other person. They will not let you have any friends. If you try to have a friend, he will insult them and embarrass them until they are not a friend anymore.

I could never admit to my Mother what I was going through, and I could never move back home. She would never say "I told you so because I already knew it."

I was never allowed to wear maternity because, at that time, you had to go on maternity leave, and there was no way my then-husband would let me go without work. Even in the summer, when teachers had off, he got me a job in recreation. He was never happy when I got pregnant, Now I can understand why. He did not want his girlfriend to know about it. I had such poor self-esteem, my then-husband had me convinced that I didn't deserve anything better.

The key word in all of this is CONTROL, and the then-husband has to have it with the entire family. I could understand why I had to pay for my sins, but my children did not deserve it. My then-husband made a Marine Sargent look like a sweetheart. He had no boundaries and no control over his behavior. At one time, he even blamed me for his drinking. It took 6 years in Al-Anon before someone could convince me. He drank because he was an Alcoholic. Never once in his life did he apologize to either the kids or me for all of his abuse.

All our oldest daughter wanted is for her father to love her. He just couldn't do it so she went elsewhere to find love, and she spent the rest of her life looking for it. She was married and had children, and he would still slap her in the face. The other children got by without their father. Our youngest son, Gordon, drowned in a neighbor's pool on March 20th, 1965. That far back, and the children did not have a father. I was so stupid, I did not realize it.

MY JOURNEY

My oldest daughter died January 9th, 2020 of a drug overdosed. Still looking for someone to love her. She left home after high school and lived in Ohio. She had two children I never saw, and the only time I heard from her was when she needed money. In the fall of 2019, her brother drove up to Ohio, packed up all of her things and drove her back to Clearwater. He got her a bicycle so she could go anywhere she wanted, got her glasses, and a library card. She tried to live the life she used to live. She even painted ceramics for Christmas gifts. Everyone thought she was doing so well. On January 9, 2020, she told her brother she wanted to go back to Ohio, She missed her family and friends. Her brother let her go. Apparently, her boyfriend picked her up at the airport and drove her straight to the drug dealer. She had been off of drugs for so long, the first dose killed her. She had never been able to find the love her father could not give her.

See, a family is like a baseball team. It can't be successful unless everyone plays the game.

We lived in a two and a half bedroom, one bath house our entire marriage. I did not even have a dish washer. After I had put over 120,000 miles on my car, I was allowed to get a net one. Really a used one that we bought at the auction in Lakeland.

It has been said that, if you live in a forest, you cannot see the trees. That is how it is with domestic violence. You feel that everyone lives like this, and they don't. I will never forget the time I watched on TV a couple buying a house. I was never asked if I liked anything. I had no opinion to express.

Now I know why we never had a couple for a friend. We never asked people over, and no one ever asked us over No woman ever wanted to be around my then-husband because he would always say something to hurt them or embarrass them. So they avoided him.

I have often wondered if he treated his girlfriend. mistress, whore or whatever you call them now, like he treated us. Somehow, I do not think so, After he got through beating us up, he could always get her comfort.

We lived in a two and a half bedroom house with one bathroom for six people our entire marriage. I did not even have a dish washer. After I had put over 120,000 miles on my car, I was not allowed to get a new one. I had to go to the auction in Lakeland and buy a used one. It never dawned on me that I deserved a new one.

It has been said that, if you live in a forest, you cannot see the trees. That is how it is with domestic violence. You feel that everyone lives like this, and they don't. I will never forget the time I watched on t.v. a couple buying a house. The wife was asked if she liked it or not. I was never asked if I liked anything. I had no opinion to express.

Now I know why we never had a couple for a friend. We never asked people over, and no one ever asked us over No woman ever wanted to be around my then-husband because he would always say something to hurt them or embarrass them. So they avoided him.

I have often wondered if he treated his girlfriend. mistress, whore or whatever you call them now, like he treated us. Somehow, I do not think so, After he got through beating us up, he could always go to her for comfort.

THE STRANGER NEXT DOOR

Y ou think you know me,

But you don't.

I have lived next door for years, but you never knew about the beatings my husband did to me, and to my children.

It may be a generational "thing" because the subject was never mentioned. I was too ashamed and embarrassed. When we were taken to the hospital, my husband always drove us and told the attendants what had happened so there was no cause of concern about domestic violence.

My husband was physically, mentally and emotionally in his beating. Of course, he was an alcoholic and blamed me for his drinking. It took six years in al-anon to realize it was not my fault he drank. He drank because he was an alcoholic.

This was not the way my life was supposed to be. We were both professionals, teachers, and no teacher would beat his children or his wife, but he did.

If you were to ask any woman why they stay in such a violent situation, each one would have a different reason. I was a perfect candidate because I had poor self-esteem, and if you can imagine it, there were times I believed I deserved it!

Before you condemn me for my actions, ask yourself if you have ever lived with someone you are afraid of? I did, for over twenty-three years. I was not allowed to have friends or a support system to share my problems with.

It took several years, after the divorce, before I could reflect on why I stayed, and even today, I do not understand. No man has a right to hit his wife and his children. The key word here is "control". He had to have control, and we had to do what he said because we knew what would happen if we did not mind him.

At one point, he encouraged me to get my masters' degree, and I was excited. This would mean, I would be spending the summers away from home. I did not know it at the time, but this was his way of getting rid of me for three months so that he could be with his whore (girlfriend, mistress, whatever, you call them.) When I came home and wanted to apply for a job, as a supervisor, because there would be more pay, he told me I could not apply. I had a job at home, and I could not be working until 5 o'clock every day. Control. Of course, this decision affected my pay all the way through retirement. He even begrudged me a raise in pay and more freedom in my career.

Now, I can see that we would have all been better off if we had left. He used us as "free slaves" and saw that we worked all the time. But then, we were all working for a better future. Work hard, save your money. And good things will happen. That is how we were trained.

People will ask: "why did you stay?" It is very difficult to leave when someone, who weighs 225 pounds standing in the way. Even when I had locked the bedroom door and put the cedar chest behind it, he still knocked the door down. That is raw anger. You have never experienced fear until something like that happens to you. And the restraining order did not work either.

During the divorce, when it came time to share our earnings, everything was gone. Hidden in other names, under other accounts. Somewhere it could not be found. So he was an abuser, a liar and a thief. I told him I could understand stealing from me, but how does a father steal from his children? He had no answer.

The story does not need to be long for it to be a lesson to other young girls who still have a chance to start over. You do not need to put up with this abuse. You do not need to let your husband tell you what to do. There are resources you can use now that I did not have.

I can only hope that someone will learn the lesson from me and be willing to go alone, by yourself, rather than continue to be dragged down by your husband.

Of course, he never told me that he had a whore on the side. She knew that he was married, but it did not matter. That is the thing about adultery. It is very selfish. You do not think about the family or the children, and how others will suffer. You think only of yourself. Even after the divorce, he denied having an affair. He is was a pathological liar.

The family has paid the price for his affair, his abuse, his stealing and his lying. But we all know the truth now. And, thank god, we are finally free of him

My biggest regret is that the children grew up without a father, and that I did not do more to protect the children. They deserved a better life. They deserved to have a father, but the adulterer thinks only of himself.

The stranger next door.

THE BATTERED WIFE

You think you know me. You sit next to me in church. I sing in the choir. I am your child's teacher. But you do not know me at all. You do not see the bruises under the eyes or the black and blue marks on the arms. The broken foot is explained by "falling off the ladder". The battered wife can explain everything. We are asked why we tolerate this kind of treatment, and our answers vary as much as the individual who suffers them. Even today, I still cannot understand why I stayed so long.

A lot of books have been written about battered wives and domestic violence. Apparently, it is a phenomenon that few can comprehend. One of the outstanding commentaries of the O.J. Simpson trials was the acknowledgment of the physical and emotional abuse that his wife has endured throughout the marriage. How could someone so attractive tolerate such abuse from her husband? This is another symptom of abuse. The smiling husband as if to cover up the abuse by saying: "who, me, I would never do such a thing". There are other symptoms of abuse: isolation, no friends, shame. Somehow, you convince yourself that "others will not know". Somehow, you will hide it.

Like a lot of other women, I have spent my lifetime in an abusive marriage thinking that I owed it to my children to have a "family" with a father and a mother, thinking that I could not survive on my own, thinking that I would, somehow, change my husband, thinking that I had failed if I sought a divorce. I married at a time when divorce was unacceptable. The family would actually ostracize you if you got a divorce. Thank goodness, young women today are provided with support groups to help them survive.

MY JOURNEY

Sarah Ban Breathnach states in her book SOMETHING MORE: "In our most precious relationships, we trust the other person enough to reveal our most innermost selves." You never have this relationship with someone who abuses you. You hide your most inner thoughts and feelings.

So, why do we stay? We stay because of the family, the children and social mores. We stay because of shame. We stay because of all the wrong reasons. After the divorce finally comes, the children will never forgive their mother for staying even though the mother thought she was doing "what was best." You stay because of the school year, the baseball season, the family vacation. You stay because you are made to feel guilty and to blame for the failure of the marriage. You stay because you really believe that things will get better if: you cook better, dress nicer, children behave better. Yes, everyone in the family becomes convinced that it is their fault.

Of course, the abusive husband knows he can have complete control. He wouldn't have married you if he didn't know that. In fact, he sought you out because he could control you.

As the time goes by, the wife realizes she has stayed too long. The children grow up and manifest all of the failures in their behaviors: running away from home (to escape the abuse), pregnancy, suspensions from school, no friends (they are not allowed to bring friends home), skipping school, lying about everything. Finally, the wife realizes she has stayed too long. There will be prices that she will have to pay to leave, but they do not seem so important anymore: loss of income, loss of financial security, loss of a place in the community, but she has already lost that and much more.

So, to survive, I had to leave the marriage. I could no longer stay for the children, the family, social mores. I had to leave to take care of me. When you are afraid to go to sleep at night and want so much to live free, it becomes necessary to leave the marriage. So much of my life has been spent looking for someone else to make me happy when, all along, I was really just seeking another me. I am responsible for making myself happy. This is a big step. Learning how to take care of ourselves. It means starting all over even if you are in your 40's, 50's even 60's. It is never too late to learn how to love yourself. In the end, we all yearn to find that one soul who will love us unconditionally for the rest of our lives.

Father Theodore Hesburgh, longtime president of the University of Notre Dame said: "The most important thing a father can do for his children is to love their mother." There is no love in a family where there is domestic violence.

After all of these years since the divorce, I still do not know or understand why I stayed in the marriage for so long. The time has helped to heal the wounds and to gain confidence in myself. Of course, the children are still paying the price for living in an abusive home. But, I realize now, I cannot continue to protect them. Somehow, they will find their own support groups, their own friends, their own place in the community. I have apologized so many times to them. It doesn't change anything. I am sorry that I put them through such a horrible childhood, but, at that time, I really didn't know any better myself. I couldn't even save me.

My oldest daughter spent her whole life trying to get the love of her father. She could never get it so she spent the rest of life trying to get it from other men. She made some bad choices. On January 9, 2020 she died from an overdose of drugs. She just could not go on living the life she had.

TRYING TO UNDERSTAND

I have spent the last few years trying to understand my feelings as stated in my book My Journey. In the chapter "The Me That I Am", I state:

"I taught school, but I was never a schoolteacher,
I had five children, but I was never a mother,
I played tennis, but I was never a tennis player,
I write, but I am not a writer."

What could I possibly mean with those statements? I remember well the guilt I had for working and being away from home. I wonder if women who work today still have the same guilty feelings? No matter where I was, I felt I "should" be somewhere else. I notice that even today I still have the same feelings. And I do not know why. When I am in a meeting, I am thinking what I will be doing afterwards. When I am sitting in church, I am making a list of things to do afterwards. I have never taken the time to "live in the now". This is really bad. I need to be focusing on the sermon and devoting that time in worship.

I think I am, finally, beginning to understand my behavior. I am reading The Dance of the Dissident Daughter by Sue Monk Kidd, and she describes some of the behaviors as: "Even as an adult woman, I'd set up perfectionist standards, which kept me striving. I pursued a thin body, happy children, an impressive speech, and a perfectly written article with determination to succeed, but also with an internal voice that led me to feel whatever I did wasn't quite enough. I worried about not measuring up." .....

"Herein lies the torment of it: Favored Daughters strive for their worth, piling up external validations, but inside they are most often plagued by self-doubt, wondering if their work or their efforts are good enough.".....

"In every one the woman is sitting in the bleacher (or the pew, the school desk, wherever) just being her girl-self when the moment of truth descends kerplunk! at her feet–that in this family, this church, this culture, female is the less-prized gender. She starts to feel that her gender has somehow 'dropped the ball." And without even being aware of what she's doing, she may try to make up for it by going through life trying to win love, validation, and esteem from the father-world."....

"I began to reflect on the ways I'd withheld my opinions, muzzled disconcerting truths, refrained from expressing my true feelings, squelched my riskier ideas, or thwarted my creativity. When I did that, I was living out the script of the Silent Woman."....

Kidd goes on to say: "Yet anger needs not only to be recognized and allowed; like the grief, it eventually needs to be transformed into an energy that serves compassion. Maybe one reason I had avoided my anger was that like a lot of people I had thought there were only two responses to anger: to deny it or to strike out thoughtlessly. But other responses are possible. We can allow anger's enormous energy to lead us to acts of resistance against patriarchy. Anger can fuel our ability to challenge, to defy injustice. It can lead to creative project, constructive, behavior, acts that work toward inclusion. In such ways anger becomes a dynamism of love."

And I did it all without knowing what I was doing. I knew that somewhere, deep inside of me, hid the me that I really am. It is not an easy thing to change one's behavior. I am trying to "live in the moment". But I find myself making grocery lists, route patterns for driving to my next errands, dreaming of going somewhere instead of just taking in my surroundings and appreciating my environment.

It is said that women are multi-tasked. We can talk on the phone, feed the baby, and stir the pot on the stove. Now, we are told that this is not a good thing. We need to focus on the task at hand. Somehow, the me that I am got lost along the way surrounded by alcoholism. It is not an excuse. It is an explanation of the why that I am. I knew that I was angry, but I did not know why. Now, I can understand the background that made "me" the "me" that I am.

It is a process. I am just trying to learn how to live a better and a more happy life. This process will go on the rest of my life. I find myself attending Al-Anon meetings. However, in the four to five years I have belonged, I have never opened up myself to anyone else in the group. I do not call any of the members to talk with them. So I am still surrounding myself with a wall so that no one can come in and see "me".

PREMONITION

The dictionary states that a premonition is: "a strong feeling that something is about to happen, esp. something unpleasant."

My definition of premonition is: "unusual behavior that cannot be explained based on inaccurate data causing a strange feeling in the gut."

Sometimes, these are small and can be discarded out of the life style. However, some cannot be ignored, and they continue to cause pain.

I had a very strong premonition in 1997 when my daughter's family had gone to Colorado without me because I had to have radiation that summer. I could not sleep, and I had the strangest feeling that they were somewhere on the side of a mountain. I could, literally, see them in a car. So I called for what seemed hours and there was no answer.

Since I had worked at the YMCA of the Rockies where they were staying, I called the operator and had our security guard go out to their cabin and check on them. I stayed on the telephone until he called back in that there were no lights on in the cabin, but it looked as if they had simply gone away leaving everything there.

While the security guard was there, the family drove up in the car and was shocked to see the cabin in bright lights flashing on it by the security car. My son-in-law's first comment was: "well, I guess your Mother is looking for us".

MY JOURNEY

This was not normal behavior, and it was not provided with accurate data, but I responded because of a premonition.

On our trip to Italy this summer, I had another premonition. It was a horrible feeling in my gut that we were going to miss our airplane to go home. It started about midnight, and I could not sleep. (I really never sleep too much before going on a trip.) But this sleeplessness would not go away. At 2 a.m. I got up and got dressed thinking I would be ready when it got time to get up.

We were to get up at 5 a.m. and leave for the train station at 5:30 a.m. I always try not to wake up my cousin who has been blessed with the ability just to "go to sleep". However, this time she turned over in the bed and asked me "what are you doing?' I said I was getting dressed so that I would be ready when we got up.

Gigi just sat up in the bed as if to give up on me. I suggested that we could go on to the airport and check in and sleep there. That way we would not miss our plane. Later on, Gigi told me it would useless to try and talk me out of it since I had my mind set. (Remember, unusual behavior based on inaccurate data.)

So, we both got up. Finished packing and went down to the lobby to check out. The hotel had a clerk on the front desk 24 hours a day who had to unlock the front door so we could leave.

Now you have to understand that my cousin, Gigi, never, never gets upset. As we walked down the street at 2:30 a.m. her only comment was: "I had really dreaded walking down these streets at 5:30 a.m. But this is even worse."

As we approached the train station, we came across between 5-10 homeless men sleeping on the side of the station. That didn't

PREMONITION

upset me very much because I knew we would be safe inside the station. Well, when we started to enter, we found out that the train station was locked up. Never one to give up, I walked across the street to a hotel and asked the clerk if we could come in until the station opened. With hand signals and a loud voice, he convinced me that he couldn't do it. (He didn't explain why.) So I walked down to another hotel and asked the same question and got the same answer.

Ever the diligent, I walked around the corner of the station and waved to the policeman behind the desk inside. He informed me that the station would not open until 5:30 a.m. and for me to leave. When I didn't move, he took his hands almost as if to say, "shoo, shoo," like you would a dog. I told him I was concerned about the men out on the street. He just continued to "shoo" me. By this time, Gigi said we had better leave or he could have us arrested. I could almost see the headlines "retired teacher arrested in Rome." So, we went back around the corner and down the street from the homeless people.

We spotted several workers waiting at a bus stop. Thank goodness, signs of life. So, we walked over in this direction to stand by them. It looked as if there was a coffee shop that had opened up at that time. Great! We can go in there and sit. By this point, I had no idea of time. I just knew I was in deep trouble with my cousin who was choosing not to speak to me. I got her some coffee and tried to make conversation, but I could see in the back of her mind she was thinking: "I could still be in bed." After a while, I see that the back door of the coffee shop is open, and it goes out into the train station. So I walked out the door and start walking, when a security guard comes by me and tells me to go back into the coffee shop.

MY JOURNEY

I have to admit that time didn't really mean much at this point. It was too early to buy a USA Today that I always buy to keep up with the news at home. It is too early to do anything. Eventually, the train station opened so we walk in and go into another coffee shop and stay until it is time to board the train.

The airport is about half an hour away.....not too bad. Arriving at the airport, we are told that we will need to board a bus to the terminal for international travel. I do not remember this coming over, but Gigi does so we go back outside and board a bus. When we arrive at Terminal C for international travel, we go directly to the Delta Crown Room so we can eat breakfast and get more coffee. By this time, I feel as if I have put in a day's work so I go right for a screwdriver. I am well past coffee.

As the time came to board the airplane, we go to the gate. I remember I have some euros and do not want to bring any home with me. At the duty free store, there is a line and only one person at the cash register. I was sure that time was not a problem, after all we started at 2:30 a.m. I visit with everyone in line and need 50 cents more to make my purchase so someone lends me the money. I walk out the door and start looking for my gate. My cousin is screaming at me and the flight attendant was standing beside her. They are closing the doors and will take off without me. Didn't I hear all of the announcements over the loud speakers. No, I couldn't hear them in the shop, and I had not told my cousin which shop I was going into because I wondered through several. They had told Gigi that she would have to remove her luggage, too, if I did not board the plane. She was furious. I have never seen her so mad. And I had no idea that I was about to miss the plane.

So my biggest fear had come true. I had almost missed the flight home.

P.S. While I was thinking about the kids in Colorado, they had been driving across the mountain. My son-in-law was driving to the other side of the state to take the kids on the train going up to Silverton, but he did not realize that you cannot make the time going across the mountain that you can on an interstate so they turned around and came back to the YMCA. So that premonition was true.

DOMESTIC VIOLENCE

Domestic violence is alive and well, and lives next door

Some characteristics of domestic violence:
1. The husband has complete control of the family.
2. the wife is not allowed to have any friends (who might provide support).
3. everyone in the family is expected to work and turn over their money to the father. (to invest, he says).
4. the wife is not allowed to wear maternity clothes because, then, she would have to go on maternity leave and no pay.
5. learn how to "make do" raise 4 children in a two-bedroom, one bath house until you really have to add one small room for a bedroom.
6. realize that if you call the police, you will really get a beating. Take out a restraining order, he does not have to obey.
7. He always drove us to the hospital so he could explain the broken foot, broken arm, black and blue marks, black eyes.
8. I drove a car with over 220,000 miles on it while he got a new driver ed car every year.

Manipulator and controller:
1. never has to tell you where he is going, or when he is coming home.
2. threaten to kill me if I ever tried to divorce him, and drove me out of the house with a gun.
3. While we were being abused physically, mentally, and emotionally, he had a whore on the side for over 23 years. Of course, he always had a lie to fix that one.
4. he never provided the court with a financial statement. Always had a way around it.

5. her husband gave her a divorce immediately. Whereas, my husband dragged it out for seven years while he, and his girlfriend changed all of the assets and put it under other names. Only his girlfriend knows where the money is.
6. He told me to take the kids and go to his mother's in indiana where I could take classes and get my masters and get a better paying job. Well, I finished in two summers, and when I went to get a better paying job, he told me I couldn't because I needed to be home taking care of the children.
7. For five of the seven years getting a divorce, I taught night classes at the junior college to pay for our daughter's college education.

In the end, he and his girlfriend (whore) took all of the money that we had worked so hard to earn. She knew it was stolen money. All I want if my half of all the money I earned (and the children's). We all worked hard and did without to save the money to have now. But, somehow, he managed to steal it and had it all under a different name. It took him seven years to do it. He can keep the money he stole from me, but I would like the see the kids get the money they worked so hard for. Only his wife know where the money is.

Pathological liar. You have to have this skill for everything else to work.

My advice would be for anyone who sees domestic violence, contact the police. You may save someone's life. I wish someone had saved mine.

I AM WOMAN HEAR ME ROAR

Several years ago, Helen Readdy made that song very popular. Maybe we should still be singing it today.

As women, we haven't been able to roar for very long. In fact, before 1970 women's history was rarely the subject of serious study.

Today women's history month celebrates the accomplishments and obstacles the female gender have overcome.

Hard to believe, but in the past women were treated as chattel and at the most, second class citizens undeserving mention in history books. Seen as inferior to men, voting, owning property or even speaking in public was frowned upon.

It took women's suffrage–women marching, picketing, protesting, going to jail–just to get our right to vote. This has not been so long ago that women got the right to vote. In fact, it was my grandmother's generation. Many forget the sacrifices that women made to get the vote.

The 60's and feminism brought big changes for women. Finally, in 1981, the united states congress passed a resolution declaring the week of march 8th as women's history month. The week grew into a month with march 8th the international women's history day.

It was the women's movement in the 1960 that played an important role in the fight for women to be recognized as valuable citizens. When I first married, even though I held down a full time job with a salary of my own, I could not buy a piece of property or open a credit card without my husband's signature! Hard to believe, isn't it?

MY JOURNEY

All of the privileges that women take for granted today did not come easily. Women began questioning why they had been held down under the thumb of men. Proclaiming discrimination and demanding equal rights, women were finally heard loud and clear.

Before the year 1970, few serious studies were conducted regarding women. As a footnote or mentioned in passing, the lives of women ere considered unimportant by male historians. Since women were not a part of the political or war machines, we factored very little into history.

When women became involved, the focus went from the male-dominated politics to american life as a whole that included urban and rural life, public health, wealth and poverty, and the media. Things that were important to women like child care and health.

No longer was it politics as usual. Women wanted to talk about important things like raising children, pregnancy, education, marriage and sexuality. They wanted to discuss racial and economic circumstances, poverty, homelessness. Today nearly every university and college offers a women's studies program. Some even offer a Ph.D.

Sonoma county california represents the birthplace of women's history month. In 1978 a public celebration was held. Senator orrin hatch and barbara mikulski so-sponsored a resolution and women's history month became a reality.

What can you do to help continue the celebration of women's history month:
1. Commemorate women's history by teaching and learning. Discuss Women's History Month with your children and with your friends.
2. Help other women. Search for a place to volunteer your services. Volunteer at a hotline helping women in abusive relationships. Be a big sister. Offer advice in your field of expertise with legal or financial problems.
3. Attend a women's sporting event. A special thanks for title ix which was passed by congress in the '70's which provides women with an equal opportunity to participate in college sports and earn scholarships. This bill was especially important to me because I went to college before it was passed. Therefore, I did not have an opportunity.
4. Watch a movie geared toward women with your friends or with your daughter. *Elizabeth I, The Golden Years, Gone with the Wind*, are just a few.
5. Say thank you. Write a heartfelt letter and send it to a woman who mentored you or inspired you in your younger years. Take your mother out to lunch and enjoy the woman she is. Celebrate the joys of being female together.
6. Head for a museum that focuses on women.
7. Throw a 'celebrate women' party. Invite friends and your sisters for a dinner or go to a great restaurant. Each person read a quote they bought and offer topics to debate and discuss.
8. Contact your government. Yes, take the time to write your local representatives or congressmen about the issues that involve women. They do take an interest.
9. You are a very valuable voter. If every woman in America would vote, they could carry every election.
10. Pay equity bill signed by Obama this year.
11. You are a very valuable human being, never forget it.

FRIENDS AND RELATIONSHIPS

This one is easy to write about. It can be said in four words: "I don't have any. Growing up on the top of the mountain, we didn't have any neighbors. When we moved into town, we were not allowed to play with any of the other children. My father must have had a phobia about anyone or anything. It was probably the result of his alcoholism. He was afraid of "outsiders". Very similar to the behavior of the mountain people you see in the movies. Growing up in such an isolated environment, it isn't any wonder that my brother and I grew up as we did. I handled it by becoming an extreme introvert. My brother handled it by being the class clown. (We both failed in how to handle the problem.)

In elementary school, we were not allowed to have any friends, and I doubt if either off us ever considered having anyone come over to our house and play. My Mother was able to have some social life in church. However, that part of her life never came into our home. It was completely separate from our family life. After the sheltered life in elementary school, neither one of us was prepared for public junior high. My brother got attention by acting out in class. I just withdrew more into myself. The entire three years in junior high I knew three girls. Imagine. Three girls. Pat Spencer, Faye Smart and Bonnie something. They were never invited to my house. Pat Spencer was the daughter of the Presbyterian minister. She knew where I lived, but she was never invited to my house. I did go to her house to play. Thank goodness, I had a physical education teacher influence me and got me involved in athletics. This was a big turning point in my life. Even though I participated in sports, I never got to know any of the other girls. I had already started building an invisible wall around me to protect me from getting hurt.

MY JOURNEY

We grew up in the part of town that would be called now the "inner city" or the "ghetto". The city of Chattanooga had city parks located throughout the city that provided activities for the young people. A lot of the other children in our neighborhood spent their days on the playground. Somehow, we formed a group of kids that spent a lot of time on the tennis courts. I'm sure the parents were relieved that we were just staying out of trouble. I Have been told that I started playing competition tennis at the age of 8. Here again, my memory has blanked out much of my childhood. I know that my Mother wanted a better life for my brother and me, and she pushed us always to "do more" or "be better". And we did achieve success on the tennis courts. I remember several of the people I played tennis with, but I would not count them as friends. And when we moved away, or went away to college, I did not keep in touch with any of them. We played in tennis tournaments, received rankings, and went on our way. The boy next door, Louis Royal, went on to become the tennis coach at the University of Tennessee. Another one went on to become the pro at the Lookout Mountain Club. (a very ritzy club). Roscoe Tanner played there.

In our three locations in Chattanooga, we were never more than half a mile away from the previous house. By the time I got to high school, I was even more conscious of where I lived and the environment, I lived in. So, I built the wall around me even more securely. My parents would come to my tennis matches, but I do not remember them coming to the school sporting events. They may have attended my brother's baseball games. To this day, I do not like baseball games, and I think it is because I associate it with alcoholism. My father never went to a baseball game (The Chattanooga Look-outs) without coming home drunk. I can still see him stumbling down the street.

FRIENDS AND RELATIONSHIPS

There was one girl in high school who actually knew where I lived and still was my friend. She lived on Oak Street and yet it was as if she lived far away because our lives were so different. She lived in a nice house and wore really nice clothes and was very popular in school. Her name was Virginia Milam and she was always my friend. When she graduated from high school, she married one of the richest men in Chattanooga, but she was always nice to me. When her two-year-old grandson drowned, she called me because she remembered I had gone through the same thing. When she flew to St. Petersburg to have surgery, she called me and invited me down to the Don Cesar Hotel where she was recuperating. She had flown down in their airplane! When meeting them, you would never know that were rich. They were down-to-earth. Her Mother made all of her clothes which were beautiful. Since we could not afford to buy clothes, Mrs. Lawson made all of my clothes. They were nice, but not beautiful.

I have no desire to return to high school reunions because I do not know anyone. I also have no desire to return to college reunions either.

Even today, I do not have many friends or relationships. During my marriage, my husband kept me away from anyone who could have been a friend by insulting or cutting me down. Later, during analysis, I learned that this is the way someone controls you, by not allowing you to have any support system. It finally got to the point where I did not want to go anywhere with him which is what he really wanted anyway. I look back now and see things much more clearly.

I have belonged to the American Association of University Women for over 20 years, and I have thoroughly enjoyed my work there. But I do not have any friends there. I retired from teaching after 30 years, but when I walked out the door, I have never been back.

MY JOURNEY

I have been able to keep in touch with six teachers that I worked with, but four of them had left the school before I retired.

I played tennis for almost 20 years with the same group every Thursday night and Saturday morning. When I had to quit because of an injury, only one of them kept in touch and that is Lois Johnson.

My granddaughter thinks I have a lot of friends because I "know" so many people, but I have to remind her that I only know them. I can count the number of friends on one hand if you don't count the thumb.

So my life has been pretty well programmed with work related projects and avoiding close relationships. I still feel guilty if I spend time going to lunch with anyone. I find myself still "running away" and choosing to put up barriers rather than taking the time to establish friendships. In large group meetings, I look around and put space between others and me. Even in Sunday School class, I will try and find a chair on the end so that I will not feel "boxed" in. Kind of like putting up a protective barrier which goes all the way back to my high school days—running home and hiding so that no one will know where I live. It is another way of keeping anyone from knowing the real me inside.

AMERICAN ASSOCIATION OF UNIVERSITY WOMEN

After my divorce, I wanted to focus on my personal growth. I got involved in AAUW because they encourage young girls and provided scholarships for young girls.

For the first time, girls were told that they could be "something more". We developed workshops for girls and their parents at the middle schools. We figured we could reach out and help develop the girls before they started high school. It was called "Girls + Math + Science = SUCCESS". Several years later, National had a program they called "STEM" which followed our patterns. We held the workshops at five different middle schools.

It was a very successful program and required many volunteers. We spent $25,000 on the programs, and a lot of businesses were wonderful supporters. We provided breakfast, lunch and snacks in the Hospitality Room all day. We also provided tee shirts for every young girl. We always had over 200 girls plus their parents. The program for the parents provided information on scholarships, student loans, even the Army recruiter came in and told the girls that they would get a four year scholarship after serving in the Army. (This was an excellent opportunity for the girls.)

We had 32 speakers for the girls and about 12 for the parents. This required a lot of volunteers to do a lot of work. When we lost several members because of retirement, we had to discontinue the program after five years.

In follow-up studies, we found for the first time ever, girls elected Class President, Vice-President, Valedictorians, and other high honors that girls had never had the opportunity before. We were so proud of them.

Another factor that helped the young girls was Title IX, the federal program that provided girls with the same opportunities that boys had in sports. This meant that girls could receive athletic scholarships to college. The schools could no longer discriminate against the girls. (Some colleges tried to declare cheerleaders as a sport until they got caught!) Right there was 12-14 girls. So cheerleading was not determined to be a sport. Although, somewhere, it may have qualified. It was just that when the colleges said it was a sport, the college did not have to provide tennis, basketball, volleyball scholarships. Not fair? Right?

We continued on working with young girls at the Junior College. The program was called *Women on the Way*. A wonderful program for young girls who have gone through a divorce and need help. It is amazing how well these young girls do with some support from the community.

After many years, I had to drop out of AUW when my son-in-law passed away as a result of an accident. I felt my daughter needed my help.

AMERICAN ASSOCIATION OF UNIVERSITY WOMEN

December 4, 2012

Dear,

For over the past twenty-five years, the Clearwater Branch, American Association of University Women, has provided two scholarships for the Women on the Way Program at St. Petersburg College (formerly St. Petersburg Junior College).

The American Association of University Women is totally dedicated to promoting education for young women. We have provided scholarships for young women in high school. We have, also, fought for over 40 years to protect our young women in athletics with the Title IX program which guarantees equality in athletic scholarships for young women. Even though the bill was passed in the 1970's, we still have colleges and universities trying to get around enforcement of the bill. AAUW provides financial and emotional support for these young women. Now, we are beginning to focus on "bullying" and the influence it has on the female students. Preventing sexual harassment in the hallways of our schools is another one of our studies.

Enclosed you will find two tickets to the play DAMN YANKEES, which will be held on Thursday, March 7th, 2013. This is our only fund-raiser for our scholarships. I hope you will be able to support our program.

Sincerely,

Margaret Hyde

TRAVEL

I love to travel. I wonder if it became a form of escape from my home life. My first trip abroad was in 1969 when I traveled to Scotland with 128 high school students. Of course, it was arranged by my husband who taught at the high school with Russell Cantwell. The Cantwells were in charge of 120 students, and I was in charge of 8 students. He thought it would be good therapy for me after losing my son in a drowning accident. I took the children to Indiana to stay with their grandmother for 6 weeks. Of course, I realized later that it also gave my husband the whole summer to be with his girlfriend. He just wanted an excuse to get me away. (I found out later that he had started the relationship in 1963.) Hindsight is so much better than foresight. He encouraged me to get my Master's Degree while I was in Indiana. It took me two summers instead of the normal three because I did a year of study while in the classroom. I must have been the dumbest person alive. No wonder he was so happy to have the kids and me out of here.

GREECE

Gigi, Lois and I were invited to go to Greece with Nick and Mary Ella. We had a ball. Needless to say, we have never been invited again! Poor Nick. He had to load and unload the car for us every time we checked in and out of a hotel. What made the trip so perfect was that Nick spoke the language and knew all of the places to go. We visited Olympia, Delphi, Patmos, Corinth, Ephesus (in Turkey), and Athens. Mary Ella and Nick flew over earliar. Lois, Gigi and I flew over together. Gigi met us in Miami. We had a big problem in Frankfort because, somehow, I had gotten into the secure area without going through security. (I still do not know how). I was on one side of the glass separating the rooms, and Lois and Gigi were on the other side, and we couldn't connect. And I had all three pieces of luggage with me so I had to go up and down the stairs with one piece of luggage at a time! Someone kept telling Gigi and Lois how to go but every time they would end up back on the other side of the glass. They went around in circles! We finally got together. The funny thing was, security at Frankfort was the tightest place of all. Yet, I managed to go through it and didn't realize how I did it. We have a strict rule when we travel. You carry only one suitcase, and you do not check any luggage. That way we don't have to wait for the luggage to clear. In Frankfort, the agent told Lois that her bag was too big and would have to be checked. Naturally, we argued, but to no avail. When we got to Athens, we had to wait for her luggage to come off the airplane. I was amazed at all of the military around the airport carrying M16's and tanks all around the field.

Nick had us a hotel room right in downtown Athens. I am always amazed at how they serve cold cuts for breakfast in Europe. Not my favorite foods. But I can exist on bread and cheese. We went shopping at the Flea Market in Athens and visited the Acropolis, the Erechtheum with its Porch of Maidens and ate the most wonderful foods in the world. The next day we went to Corinth. This is where Paul wrote the letters to the Corinthians. We crossed the largest man made canal that was so beautiful, but I can't remember what two bodies of water it connected. We went to Olympia where we stayed in the most beautiful hotel. All white—inside and out. When we went to bed that night, Lois' bed collapsed. One of the planks slipped out. We died laughing. I rinsed out my underwear and hung it on the lamp to dry and it got burn marks on it. Everything dries so fast in Greece because it is so dry. Early the next morning, we discovered that they had a rooster in the yard because it woke us up. It was such a treat for everyone. Nick gave us a tour of where the first Olympic races took place. Only men participated and no women were allowed because the men were nude. On the way to Delphi, Nick was getting tired of driving and asked if anyone could drive a stick shift. Of course, I answered that I could because of all the driving in the jeep. Nick was so tired, he got into the back seat to go to sleep. However, by the time I had shifted into first gear and started to take off, Nick was wide awake. I could see his eyes wide open in the rear view mirror!

Nick knew the way to Delphi, but somehow, I got on the wrong road and we ended up going across some pretty high mountains, with very narrow roads. In fact, that was the first place I saw mirrors used to let you know if a car was coming in the opposite direction. It was also the first place we saw beautiful memorials on the side of the road. I mean they were beautiful and had glass on all four side with candles inside, painted all different kinds of colors. Naturally, I liked the blue ones best of all and said I would love to have one. Nick said that if I wasn't more careful in driving, he was going to open the door and push me out and get me one. I didn't realize that they were memorials for people who had died at that spot. (Now, we see them in the United States, but they are not as nice.) We went across a mountain where whole villages were wiped out during World War II. Now, the villages were so quiet. I had to stop to allow sheep to cross the road. It wasn't really the way to Delphi, in fact the road wasn't even on the map, but it turned out to be one of the best parts of the trip, and we did make it to the ferry to cross over to Delphi. Nick changed back to driving somewhere along the way, and we were so low on gas, we were afraid we wouldn't make it to the next gas station. Nick coasted as much as possible. When we finally reached a gas station, everything was closed for siesta. I got out of the car and went and knocked on the door. Thank goodness, a man came out and filled the tank. I was told that it wasn't nice to wake someone up during siesta, but that was nothing compared to running out of gas!

After we got the gas, we started looking for a bathroom. We found some public bathrooms so Nick told Lois, Gigi and me to go on down. He and Mary Ella would wait. When we got to the bottom of the stairs and saw the bathrooms just had holes in the ground, we ran back out. Nick and Mary Ella just stood at the top of the stair and laughed to see how long it would take before we ran back up the stairs. We told them we would just wait. We didn't need to go either.

The ship going over to Delphi was really nice and neat. It was a beautiful clear day and the sky was so blue. Delphi is the center of the universe to the Greeks. Our hotel room over-looked the side of the mountains. I found an old vase in the alley that had been thrown away, and I hand carried it all the way home. Cheryl, at Colonial Florist, put a lovely dry flower arrangement in it. Even though it was cracked, it is one of my favorite flower arrangements.

On the way back to Athens from Delphi, while going through some heavy road construction, Nick switched back into the center lane, and we didn't think anything about it. We heard a policeman's whistle, but we thought it was for someone else so we told Nick to just go on driving. Several miles down the road someone passed us and yelled out that there was a police car chasing us. Nick pulled over, and I don't know if it was because Nick could speak the language or what, but the policeman really yelled at him. It was bad. I got out my video camera to take pictures, but the others told me to get back in the car. I didn't think they would yell so much if the policeman knew I was taking pictures. I was told that the policeman would take my camera if I tried to take pictures. I was sure we would have won a prize on America's funnies videos with the pictures, but I didn't want to lose my camera with all of the pictures I had in it. Afterwards, Nick said he wished I had taken the pictures for him to use in court. I wish I had, too.

When we got back to Athens, we boarded a boat to Samos. Now, we could have taken a hydroplane or a boat. It was cheaper to go by boat. Turned out to be the "milk boat", I think Nick called it. Anyway, the trip took a really long time and it was about 3 am when we arrived in Samos. The boat stopped at every island, and I really enjoyed the trip. I called it our island trip because we got to see so many different islands. I tried to count the number of churches on the islands, but there were too many. One time, I think I counted 14. On Samos, we went to the most beautiful restaurant. We had to go by bus, so Nick told the bus driver where to let us off. Well, for some strange reason, we got dropped off a long distant from the restaurant. There were the five of us all walking in a line down the side of the road. We called it Nick's "harem"

While we were in Samos, Gigi, Lois and I took a side trip to Ephesus which is in Turkey. Nick and Mary Ella had already been so the girls had to go by themselves. We had to cross over on a ferry boat which was neat. However, on arriving in Ephesus, we had to surrender our passports until we boarded the ferry that night to return back to Samos. That is a weird feeling, to be in Turkey and not have a passport. Ephesus is a beautiful town. It has the oldest library in the world. It is also where Paul preached and had to be taken, under cover, out of the amphitheater to avoid persecution. It is also where Paul preached so long in someone's house that a man fell out of the upstairs window. They had perfect public baths with running water via an aqueduct. The slaves would sit on the open seats to get them warm for their masters. The Greeks and Romans both realized how important water was long before anyone else.

After Samos, we traveled to Kow which is another beautiful island. We got to see where the chariots had worn down tracks in the granite rocks. The fruits and vegetables were so good in Greece, but I especially remember the figs on Kow and the bougainvilleas growing everywhere!

I think one of the best trips was to Meteora. The monks live on the top of the mountains, and all of their food and water had to be put in baskets and pulled up by the monks. The monks lived in caves, and they felt they were closer to heaven. I have to agree. However, now they have cut steps up to the top so visitors can climb up to the top. This is where they filmed the commercial for Spirit shoes. I think anyone who goes to Greece should go to Meteora. Our hotel was so brand new that we were one of the first guests. A lot that I had typed about Greece is gone. I do not know when we went o Meteora, but I think it was on the way up to Delphi.

It was a WONDERFUL trip and spoiled us for all of the trips we took afterwards. Nick and Mary Ella took such good care of us. We could never have done it all without Nick and Mary Ella! At the time, I was working as a travel agent so I kept records of all of our expenses. The two-week trip cost $1,328.00 and that included our airfare! We also flew back from Kow to Athens at the end of the trip. We did a one week "land tour" and a week "island tour". We visited five historical places: Delphi, Olympia, Corinth, Acropolis in Athens, Meteora and so much more.

"THE BOYS" THAT HELPED SAVE A FAMILY

I sat beside my son-in-law's hospital bed, while he lay in a coma, and bargained with God: "Please let it be me. I have led a full life, and he is too young to go. He needs to be here because he has three beautiful children who need a father. I have lived my life. I am ready to go."

Rick Warren's book, *PURPOSE DRIVEN LIFE*, states that we are all here for a reason, and each one of us has a purpose. While God sees the whole picture, we are allowed to see only a small part of the total picture. This is a concept that I have been taught to believe, but when my son-in-law passed away, I questioned the concept. Why am I here? And I questioned God? The family walked through the "valley of the shadow of death" alone. We each one grieved so much…. we could not help each other.

Then, slowly, over a period of time, we crawled out of our deep abyss of grief and tried to walk, one step at a time, back to the surface of life.

That is when my granddaughter, who is wise beyond her years, decided to get a puppy. I was adamant, however, "if there is one thing you do not need as a college student, with your schedule and all, is a puppy!" She listened to me, just like my own children, and went out and got the puppy.

It was a tiny puppy. So small, Taylor carried it in her cotton cloth shoulder bag. I reminded her of my allergies, and the reasons why I had never had an animal in my house. "This one is different. He is hypo-allergic. You cannot be allergic to him." Taylor decided to name it KALE, after his father. The only kale I knew was the wild vegetable that grew on my grandmother's farm. So much for names! I got to name my children so I guess Taylor could name her puppy.

MY JOURNEY

My daughter, Stacy, who had never allowed dirt in her house much less a puppy acquiesced to her daughter's wishes, and Kale was welcomed into the house. In fact, my daughter fell in love with KALE so much, she got another puppy for her son. (everyone always thought it was for herself). His name would be RA-RA after some baseball player. This way the puppies would have someone to play with and not get lonely. Even though they are not biological brothers, they have been raised as brothers. They are called "the boys". Sometimes, "the boys" are at FSU with my granddaughter. Sometimes, "the boys" are at home with my daughter.

Naturally, the time would come when I would be asked to bring "the boys" to Tallahassee. Because of my concern over allergies, a neighbor came down and walked the dogs, loaded them in the back seat along with their: bed, sheets, toys, dog food, and a bowl of water on the floor. My granddaughter promised me that they would sleep the whole way to Tallahassee.

Needless to say, that is not what happened! Taylor had warned me that when KALE made a "whiny" sound, it meant he needed to go to the bathroom. We did not make 10 miles before I heard what I assumed was a "whiny" sound so I pulled over, fastened their collars with the leashes and walked them. That was a big mistake. Now, KALE knew I was an idiot and made me stop several more times before getting to Tallahassee.

Next, I was asked to come up and walk them, when they are at home in Tarpon Springs, so that they do not get "lonely" since they are by themselves from 7 a.m. 'till at least 2 p.m. (After all, what else do you have to do?) I tried walking them in the neighborhood which is difficult since "the boys" do not know the word: "no". Sometimes, they go into their "tracking mode": nose held high, front paw raised and the curly tail still curled. They do not know their tail should be straight! Then they go into their "Alaskan sled pulling" mode as if they are racing in the Iderod between Anchorage and Nome: pulling their leashes taunt, front legs kicking fast, back legs kicking up, and going nowhere. They forget the sled they are pulling is me!

Whereas most dogs "hike up" to a fire hydrant or a telephone pole, "the boys" hike up to a blade of grass or a leaf. They are ambidextrous and can "hike up" with either leg— sometimes doing it together. Of course, they are competitive. If one goes off to check something out, the other one has to "go and check it out, too." I envy other people out walking their dogs so calmly and quietly while my two are going to the opposite sides of the road, and I am in the middle. The others come home rested while I come home exhausted as if I have been in a war with "the boys" pulling me every way possible. I say that they are spoiled while my granddaughter assures me you cannot spoil a dog with love!

This was not what I had planned in my "golden twilight years". I watch my neighbors leaving for work in the morning, and I think "how wonderful" to get a coffee break and enjoy intelligent conversation with other teachers. That is pretty sad.... to envy someone who is going to work! Some are going to play a round of golf. Some are going to play tennis while I am "walking two dogs". But they make me laugh, and I enjoy "talking" with them.

It has been said that God laughs while we make plans. "The boys" have become a way of bringing our family together again. They are all we talk about. We exchange conversations all the time about what "the boys" are doing. We are learning how to live again. Of course, we are still sad, but we can laugh because we know when we come home, "the boys" will be there to greet us with unconditional love.

They came into my life, unwanted, and stayed long enough to win my heart.

PEOPLE WHO INFLUENCED ME

THANK YOU, THANK YOU, THANK YOU

I would be much remiss if I did not take the time to share with you all of the people who have taken this journey with me:

God has been with me, even during the years I turned my back to Him, I knew he was there,

My Mother, was always there pushing me to do better, be better, have a better life than she had,

My brother, Joe, who was so good-looking and could sing! When he went to Tennessee-Wesleyan, a Methodist college, he sang in the chorus and acted in musicals. His favorite song was "You'll Never Walk Alone." It still makes me sad to hear it. After four years in the Air Force, he came home an alcoholic and gambler. It was downhill from then on. (I could not sing at all!)

Miss McIntire's Day School. When the family moved off the mountain, everything we owned was in an old suitcase held together by a rope. Mother did not know that public schools, at that time, required parents to purchase all textbooks. All four of us were living in one room. She did not have money to buy any books so she walked down to Miss McIntire's Day School which was in her home. She had about 16 students first through 8th grade. As far as I know, we were her only "scholarship" students. My father was supposed to do repairs to pay for our tuition, but I never saw him there. My brother was six, and he was required to start school. Since I was the only person he knew in the world, he refused to go unless I went so I spent two years in pre-school so Joe would go to school. We started public school in the 7th grade. I was so shy, I only met two girls in the 7th grade.

Miss Stagmier, junior high P.E. teacher, who pushed me into athletics which saved my life. I would not be here today without athletics. Several kids in our neighborhood died in fights (gunfire or knives).

When my brother and I got old enough to go down to the city playground, two blocks away, my Mother got a job as playground director (so she could keep an eye on us and so she could push us into activities.) Eventually, we ended up on the tennis courts all day. We were both city champions. In fact, our playground produced 5 city champions.

Dr. James Hipp, Superintendent of our Sunday School at Trinity Methodist. He did everything possible to involve us in church activities, i.e. Sunday Church, Sunday School, Sunday evenings youth group, Wednesday night suppers. He even got my brother a tennis scholarship at Tennessee-Wesleyan which was a Methodist junior college in Athens, TN. If either one of us failed, it was not because of Dr. Hipp, he worked so hard.

Miss Bennett, high school English teacher, who made it possible for me to skip freshmen English in college.

John Hunter, who paid our tuition at the City Tennis Club. He provided 5-6 tennis players from the city playground who could not afford to join the City Tennis Club.

Alex Guerry, President of the Southern Lawn Tennis Association, and also President of the City Tennis Club, who made it possible for me to play on the Southern Lawn Tennis Team. I went to Philadelphia and played in the nationals. I don't remember how

PEOPLE WHO INFLUENCED ME

I got there. I don't remember playing there. The only thing I remember is the house where I stayed. They had two different kinds of cereal. I had never seen that before!

Charlotte Nan Jones, my room-mate who made it possible for me to be in her sorority when I was not a legacy or with a letter of recommendation. She convinced them to take me because we could win sports events which we did.

YMCA OF THE ROCKIES which provided me with the wonderful opportunity to spend 8 summers in the cool mountains. For 5 years I worked as a volunteer for room and board only. It was great. I only worked 20 hours and could attend all the lectures and workshops I wanted to. With a master's degree, I was assigned to the laundry. Another laundry worker had his PHD from Colorado. Then, I had to work for pay which involved working 40 hours a week. I think it averaged $3.25, and it was worth it! We have an annual reunion with about 10 of us, and we are still doing it 14 years later.

Teacher friends who have always provided me with support: Karen Henderson, Molly Sexton, Suzanne Erickson, Jackie McWhorter, Sharon Turner, Barbara Anderson.

Neighbors who have supported me so much with all trips to the doctors, etc. Cheryl and Roy Roggensack, Kennan and Don O'Donnell.

Rev. Landers and Triss Masters, at Heritage Methodist Church, who are just plain sweet-hearts. I can still remember Triss walking Spencer because he was crying during Sunday School. My Rock and Role Class with Chris Iaquinto and J. R. Richardson as leaders.

Gigi, my cousin, who has been like a sister to me.

My wonderful children who endured horrible cruel, sadistic treatment by their father. They deserved something better.

Now, you can understand why I have worked for over 25 years to provide scholarships to the Women on the Way program at St. Petersburg College. That is also why I raised over $25,000 to provide a program for 8th grade girls called "Girl's + Math + Science=SUCCESS". Now, it is called STEM. To guide girls into Math and Science classes.

Ingrid, my care giver, who made it possible for me to stay in my home as long as possible.

Triss Masters, at Heritage Methodist Church, an all-around walking saint She would walk Spencer during Church because he was crying.

Mary Alice Mistal, another walking around saint; I never heard her say an unkind word about anybody. And Lois Johnson, always a friend.

My three grandchildren: Taylor, Spencer and Sawyer who allowed me to be a part of their lives, and enjoy it. Something I could never do with my own children.

I wanted to give back because of all that has been given to me.

THANK YOU,
WITH LOVE,

Margaret

Jj Kk Ll Mm Nn Oo Pp Qq Rr Ss Tt Uu Vv Ww Xx Yy Zz
November 14, 2001
HOMEWORK
'94 3 7

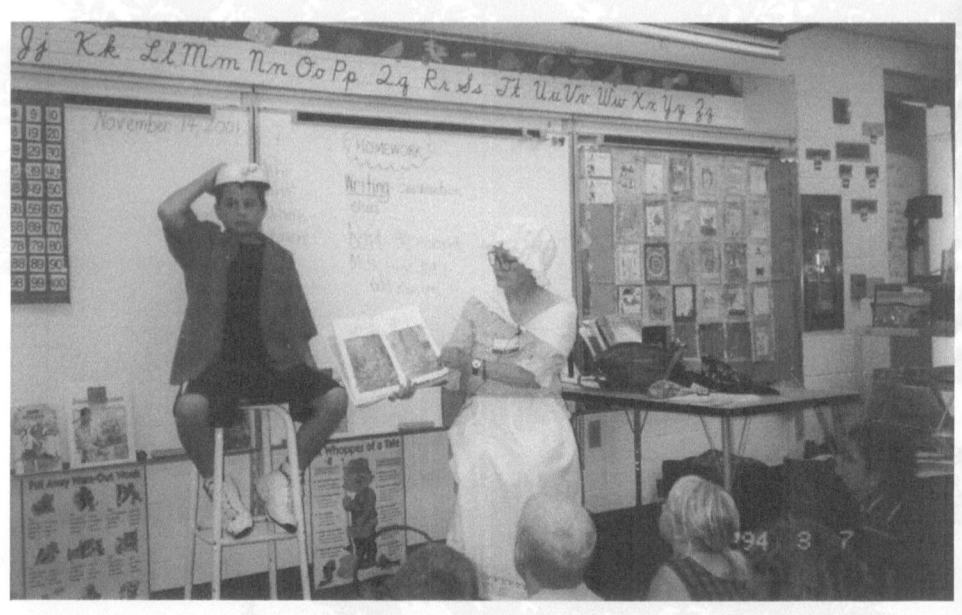

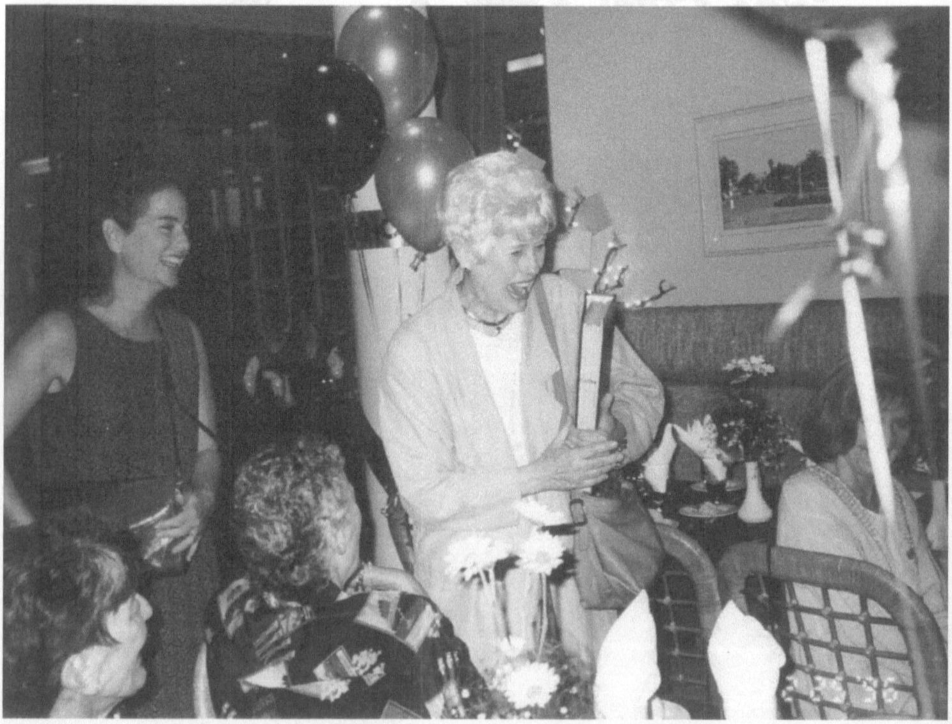

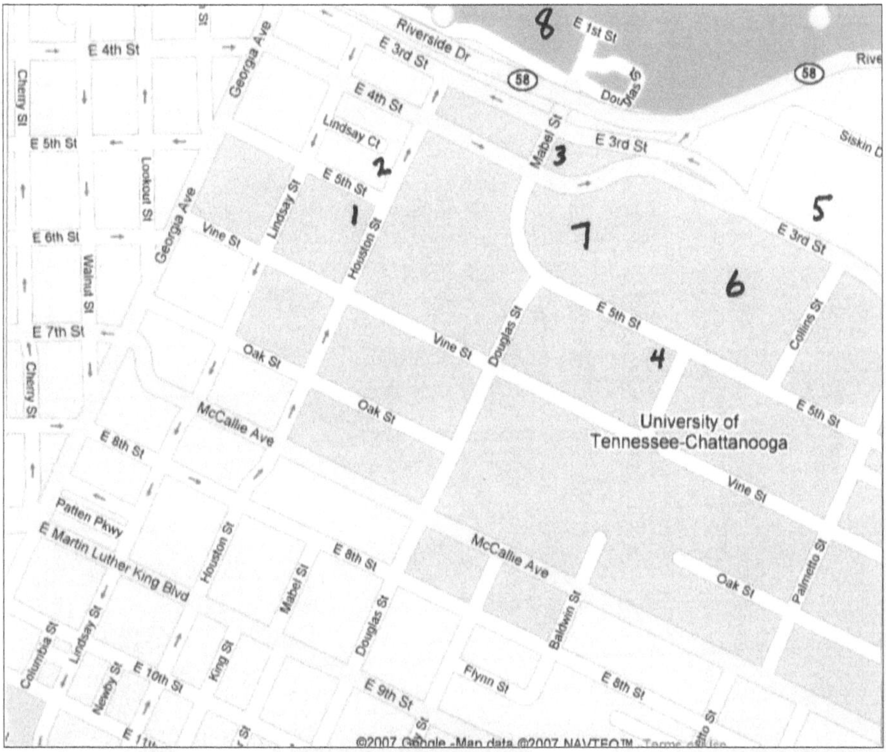
E 4th St
Cherry St
E 5th St
Lookout St
E 6th St
Walnut St
E 7th St
Cherry St
E 8th St
Patten Pkwy
E Martin Luther King Blvd
Columbia St
Lindsay St
Newby St
E 10th St
King St
Houston St
Mabel St
Douglas St
E 9th St
Georgia Ave
Vine St
Lindsay St
Oak St
McCallie Ave
E 8th St
Riverside Dr
E 3rd St
E 4th St
Lindsay Ct
E 5th St
Houston St
E 1st St
58
Mabel St
E 3rd St
Siskin D
E 3rd St
E 5th St
Collins St
Vine St
Douglas St
Oak St
E 5th St
University of
Tennessee-Chattanooga
Vine St
McCallie Ave
Oak St
Palmetto St
Baldwin St
Flynn St
E 8th St
8
2
3
1
7
5
6
4

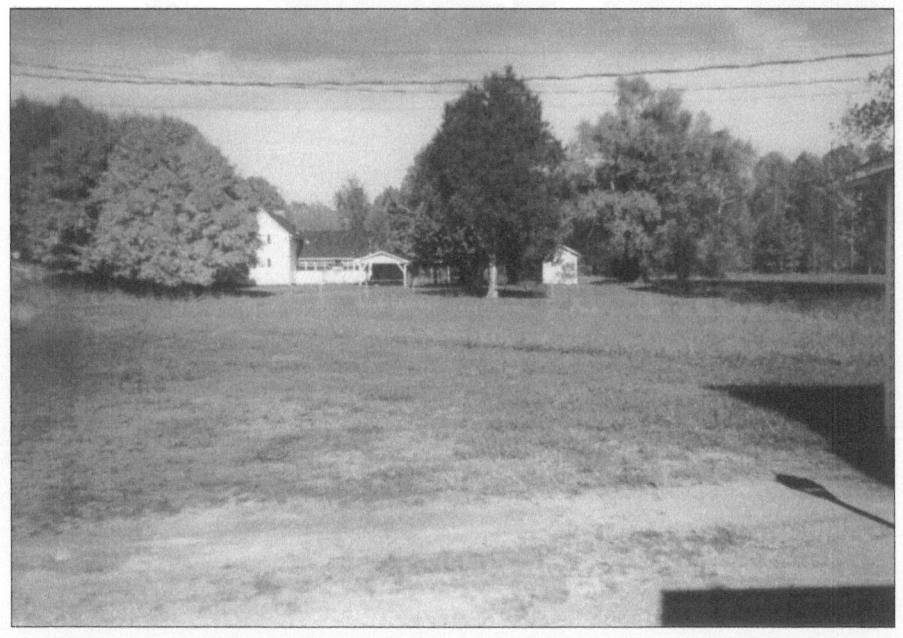

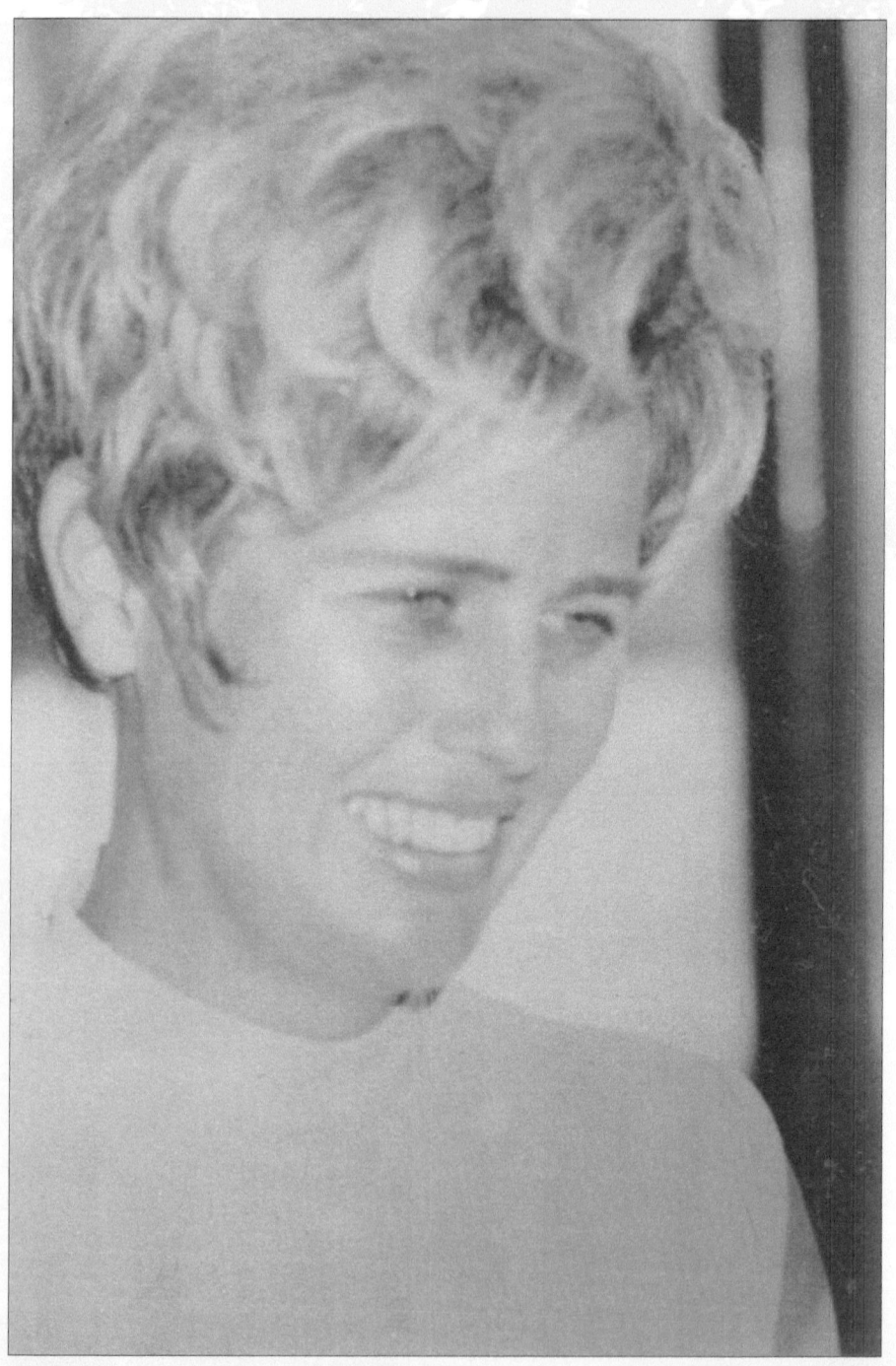

Margaret Hyde
2369 Podocarpus Way
Clearwater, FL 33759
727-797-0568
margaretwhalen2433@gmail.com